"IN ORDER TO DISCOVER YOURSELF, YOU HAVE TO BE REAL WITH YOURSELF."

— Maurice Lindsay

Printed in the United States of America

First edition: December 2016.

Book cover designed by *Ugo Onah.*

ISBN: 978-0-692-80778-1

BLESSEDPRESS

An Indie Publisher of Faith-Based Books from an Urban Perspective

P.O. Box 1824, Lithonia, GA 30058

To all of my young African American brothers out there seeking to grow and become a better version of yourself, this journal is for you. Think of it as a little treasure trove to store your personal thoughts, observations, emotions and heart's desires. I think you'll find that recording the echoes of your soul on paper, will not only help you discover who you are, but give you the feedback you need to become the man whom The Most High created you to be. I pray that this journal will be a blessing to you.

Shalom!

"You are <u>a chosen race</u>; a royal priesthood, a set apart nation, a people for a possession, that you should proclaim the praises of Him who called you out of darkness into His marvellous light."

— 1 Kepha (Peter) 2:19

4

Who am I?
(Describe yourself in full detail)

They have said, "Come, And let us wipe them out as a nation, And let the name of Yisra'ĕl be remembered no more."

— Tahalym (Psalms) 83:4

Where did my family's last name come from?

(If you don't know it, research it and write about it later)

"And יהוה shall bring you back to Mitsrayim [slavery] in ships, by a way of which I said to you, 'You are never to see it again.' And there you shall be sold to your enemies as male and female slaves, but no one to buy."

— Dabarym (Deuteronomy) 28:68

How did my ancestors arrive to the Americas or Islands?

(If you don't know, research it and write about it later)

"See, I am bringing a nation against you from afar, O house of Yisra'ĕl," declares יהוה. "It is an enduring nation, it is an ancient nation, a nation whose language you do not know, nor do you understand what they say."

— Yaramyahu (Jerimiah) 5:15

What language did my ancestors speak before they arrived to the Americas or Islands?

(If you don't know, research it and write about it later)

_____

_____

_____

_____

_____

_____

_____

_____

_____

_____

_____

_____

_____

_____

_____

_____

_____

_____

"Thus you shall become an astonishment, a proverb, and a mockery among all the peoples to which הוהי drives you."

— Dabarym (Deuteronomy) 28:37

Why is my race treated so differently (harshly) than all the other races here?

And among those nations you are to find
no rest, nor have a resting place for the
sole of your foot. But there יהוה shall give
you a trembling heart, and failing eyes,
and sorrow of being.''

—Dabarym (Deuteronomy) 28:65

How does it feel to being a black man in America (or elseshere)?

_____
_____
_____
_____
_____
_____
_____
_____
_____
_____
_____
_____
_____
_____
_____
_____
_____
_____
_____
_____

"He who gets heart loves his own life; He who guards understanding finds good."

— Mashaly (Proverbs) 19:8

Do I love myself?

(Describe your relationship with yourself)

"I give thanks to You, For I am awesomely and wondrously made! Wondrous are Your works, And my being knows it well."

— Tahalym (Psalms) 139:14

What do I like about myself?
(Describe your best qualities)

_____

_____

_____

_____

_____

_____

_____

_____

_____

_____

_____

_____

_____

_____

_____

_____

_____

_____

_____

"Examine yourselves whether you are in the belief – prove yourselves. Or do you not know yourselves, that עשוהי Messiah is in you, unless you are disapproved."

—2 Qorintiym (Corinthians) 13:5

What do I dislike about myself?

(Describe your flaws)

"Become imitators of me, as I also am of Messiah."

— 1 Qorintiym (Corinthians) 11:1

Who do I admire or desire to be like?

(Who is your role model and why)

_____

_____

_____

_____

_____

_____

_____

_____

_____

_____

_____

_____

_____

_____

_____

_____

_____

_____

_____

"All that your hand finds to do, do it with your might; for there is no work or planning or knowledge or wisdom in the grave where you are going."

— Qahalath (Ecclesiastes) 9:10

What am I good at?

(Describe your gifts, talents, or special skills)

"Restore to me the joy of Your deliverance, And uphold me, Noble Spirit!"

— Tahalym (Psalms) 51:12

What makes me happy?

(Describe what activity or person brings you joy)

"For every matter there is an appointed time, even a time for every pursuit under the heavens."

— Qahalath (Ecclesiastes) 3:1

What do I spend the majority of my time doing?

(Describe what activity you do the most and why)

_____

_____

_____

_____

_____

_____

_____

_____

_____

_____

_____

_____

_____

_____

_____

_____

_____

_____

"Do not become unevenly yoked with unbelievers. For what partnership has righteousness and lawlessness? And what fellowship has light with darkness?"

— 2 Qorintiym (Corinthians) 6:14

Who do I spend the majority of my time with?

(Describe who you hang out with the most and why)

"And הוהי Elohim took the man and put him in the garden of Ĕḏen to work it and to guard it."

— Barashyth (Genesis) 2:15

Where do I spend the majority of my time at?

(Describe where you spend the most time at and why)

_____

_____

_____

_____

_____

_____

_____

_____

_____

_____

_____

_____

_____

_____

_____

_____

_____

_____

_____

"But let a man examine himself, and so let him eat of that bread and drink of that cup."

— 1 Qorintiym (Corinthians) 11:28

Is the majority of my time spent bettering my life or hindering it?

(Describe your answer)

"Let us hear the conclusion of the matter: Fear Elohim and guard his commands, for this is the duty of all mankind."

— Qahalath (Ecclesiastes) 3:1

What is my life's purpose?
(Describe what you think God put you on this Earth to do)

"Many are the plans in a man's heart, But it is the counsel of הוהי that stands."

— Mashaly (Proverbs) 13:12

What do I really want to accomplish in my lifetime?

(Describe your ultimate goals in life)

"Hope deferred makes the heart sick, but a longing come true is a tree of life."

— Mashaly (Proverbs) 13:12

Where do I want to be in life 5 years from now?

(Describe your immediate goals in life)

"The being of the lazy one craves, but has not; While the being of the hard workers are enriched."

— Mashaly (Proverbs) 13:4

Does my work ethic match my ambition?
(Describe your work habits)

"Commit your works to יהוה, And your plans shall be established.

— Mashaly (Proverbs) 16:3

What can I do now to better my life later?
(Describe what habits you need to change)

"Give thanks to יהוה! Call upon His Name,
Make known His deeds among the
peoples."

— Tahalym (Psalms) 105:1

What am I the most thankful for in life?

(Describe what you are grateful for)

"A man of many friends might come to ruin, but there is one loving one who sticks closer than a brother."

— Mashaly (Proverbs) 18:24

Who is the most important person in my life?

(Describe why they are so important)

_____

_____

_____

_____

_____

_____

_____

_____

_____

_____

_____

_____

_____

_____

_____

_____

_____

"A friend loves at all times, and a brother is born for adversity."

— Mashaly (Proverbs) 17:17

Who treats me as I'm the most important person in their life?

(Describe who and how they treat you)

_____

_____

_____

_____

_____

_____

_____

_____

_____

_____

_____

_____

_____

_____

_____

_____

_____

_____

_____

"If you have received a friend, prove him first and don't be in a hurry to credit him."

— Sirach (Ecclesiasticus) 6:7

Who are the few people that I can trust and depend on no matter what?

(Describe who and how they've earned your trust them)

"Do not forsake your own friend or your father's friend, And do not go into your brother's house In the day of your calamity — Better is a neighbor nearby than a brother far away."

— Mashaly (Proverbs) 27:10

Do the people who love me the most receive the same love back from me?

(Describe how you treat people who love you)

"Do not take vengeance or bear a grudge against the children of your people. And you shall love your neighbor as yourself. I am יהוה."

— Uyaqara (Leviticus) 19:18

Do I see other African Americans as my people or strangers?

(Describe how you view your people)

_____
_____
_____
_____
_____
_____
_____
_____
_____
_____
_____
_____
_____
_____
_____
_____
_____

"And when Abram heard that his brother was taken captive, he armed his three hundred and eighteen trained servants who were born in his own house, and went in pursuit as far as Dan."

— Barashyth (Genesis) 14:14

Do I care when I hear that something bad happens to other African Americans?

(Describe why or why not)

_____

_____

_____

_____

_____

_____

_____

_____

_____

_____

_____

_____

_____

_____

_____

_____

_____

_____

_____

"Make my joy complete by being of the same mind, having the same love, one in being and of purpose."

— Philipiyim (Philippians) 2:2

Do I wish for my people the same as I wish for myself?

(Describe why or why not)

"For you, brothers, have been called to freedom, only do not use freedom as an occasion for the flesh, but through love serve one another."

— Galatiyim (Galatians) 5:13

Do I live my life in service to others or in service to only me?

(Describe your life or service)

_____
_____
_____
_____
_____
_____
_____
_____
_____
_____
_____
_____
_____
_____
_____
_____
_____
_____
_____
_____
_____

"My little children, let us not love in word or in tongue, but in deed and in truth."

— 1 Yahuchanan (John) 3:18

What is the most memorable deed I've ever done for someone?

(Describe the deed and how it made you feel)

"Create in me a clean heart, O Elohim,
And renew a steadfast spirit within me."

— Tahalym (Psalms) 51:10

Am I pleased with who I am as a person?
(Describe how you feel about your character)

_____

_____

_____

_____

_____

_____

_____

_____

_____

_____

_____

_____

_____

_____

_____

_____

_____

_____

"If we confess our sins, He is trustworthy and righteous to forgive us the sins and cleanse us from all unrighteousness."

— 1 Yahuchanan (John) 1:19

What is one action I did that I wish I could take back?

(Describe the deed and why you regret it)

"Confess your trespasses to one another, and pray for one another, so that you are healed. The earnest prayer of a righteous one accomplishes much."

— Yahqub (James) 5:16

Is there anyone that I need to apologize to for something that I did to them?

(Describe the wrong you did)

"For if you forgive men their trespasses, your heavenly Father shall also forgive you."

— Mathathiyahu (Matthew) 6:14

Is there anyone that I have not forgiven for the wrong they did to me?

(Describe the who and why not)

"Everyone doing sin also does lawlessness, and sin is lawlessness."

— 1 Yahuchanan (John) 3:4

What is my idea of morality?
(Describe what you think is right and wrong)

"Do not be led astray, Evil company corrupts good habits."

— 1 Qorintiym (Corinthians) 15:33

Are the people in my life influencing me to live right or wrong?

(Describe how your friends influence you)

"Bring your heart to discipline, And your ears to words of knowledge."

— Mashaly (Proverbs) 23:12

Does the music I regularly listen to, influence me to live right or wrong?

(Describe your favorite music's influence on you)

_____

_____

_____

_____

_____

_____

_____

_____

_____

_____

_____

_____

_____

_____

_____

_____

_____

_____

"But above all, my brothers, do not swear, either by the heaven or by the earth or with any other oath. But let your Yes be Yes, and your No, No, lest you fall into judgment."

— Yahqub (James) 5:12

Am I a man of my word?

(Describe if people trust what you say or not)

"Follow me as I follow the Messiah."

— Qorintiym (Corinthians) 11:1

Do I expect others to do for me more than what I do for myself?

(Describe why or why not)

_____

_____

_____

_____

_____

_____

_____

_____

_____

_____

_____

_____

_____

_____

_____

_____

_____

_____

_____

"Therefore, having put off the false, speak truth, each one with his neighbor, for we are members of one another."

— Eph'siyim (Ephesians) 4:25

Do I tell the truth when people ask me questions or lie to save face?

(Describe how you normally react to people)

"Blessed are those persecuted for righteousness sake, for theirs is the reign of the heavens."

— Mathathyahu (Matthew) 5:10

Would I stand up for what I know is right if my life was on the line?

(Describe why or why not)

"He who has found a wife has found good,
And receives favor from יהוה."

— Mashaly (Proverbs) 18:22

Do I want to be married one day?

(Describe why you do or don't)

"A widow or one put away or a defiled woman or a whore — these he does not take. But a maiden <u>of his own people</u> he does take as a wife."

— Uyaqara (Leviticus) 21:14

What type of female do I want to marry?
(Describe your ideal woman)

_____
_____
_____
_____
_____
_____
_____
_____
_____
_____
_____
_____
_____
_____
_____
_____
_____
_____

"Respect your father and your mother, so that your days are prolonged upon the soil which יהוה your Elohim is giving you."

— Shamuth (Exodus) 20:12

Do I treat women how I want my mother or sister to be treated?

(Describe how you handle women)

_____

_____

_____

_____

_____

_____

_____

_____

_____

_____

_____

_____

_____

_____

_____

_____

_____

"Let the husband render to his wife what is her due, and likewise also the wife to her husband."

— Qorintiym (Corinthians) 7:3

Am I financially able to take care of a woman?

(Describe your financial situation)

"And they killed Hamor and Shekem his son with the edge of the sword, and took Dinah from Shekem's house, and went out. The sons of Ya'aqob came upon the slain, and plundered the city, because they had defiled their sister."

— Barashyth (Genesis) 34:26-27

Am I willing to protect my woman from physical abuse?

(Describe your views on defending women)

_____

_____

_____

_____

_____

_____

_____

_____

_____

_____

_____

_____

_____

_____

_____

_____

_____

_____

"For this cause a man shall leave his father and mother, and cleave to his wife, and they shall become one flesh."

— Barashyth (Genesis) 2:24

Do I feel mentally ready to be a husband or do I have some growing to do?

(Describe your maturity level)

_____

_____

_____

_____

_____

_____

_____

_____

_____

_____

_____

_____

_____

_____

_____

_____

_____

_____

_____

"Wives, subject yourselves to your own
husbands, as is proper in the Master.
Husbands, love your wives and do not be
bitter toward them."

— Qolasim (Colossians) 3:18-19

Is my current marriage/relationship a happy one?

(Describe your marriage life)

_____

_____

_____

_____

_____

_____

_____

_____

_____

_____

_____

_____

_____

_____

_____

_____

_____

_____

"Do not become unevenly yoked with unbelievers. For what partnership have righteousness and lawlessness? And what fellowship has light with darkness?"

— Qorintiym (Corinthians) 6:14

Are me and my wife/fiancé equally yoked?
(Describe each other's faith)

"Husbands, love your wives, as Messiah also did love the assembly and gave Himself for it."

— Eph'siym (Ephesians) 5:25

Am I fulfilling my duties as a husband?
(Describe your role as a husband)

"When a man has taken a new wife, let him not go out into the army nor let any matter be imposed upon him. He shall be exempt one year for the sake of his home, to rejoice with his wife whom he has taken."

— Dabarym (Deuteronomy) 24:5

What can I do to make sure that my current or future marriage is successful?

(Express your ideas)

"Look, children are an inheritance from הוהי, The fruit of the womb is the reward."

— Tahalym (Psalms) 127:3

Do I want to be a father one day?

(Describe why you do or don't)

"Children, listen to the discipline of a father, And give attention to know understanding."

— Mashaly (Proverbs) 4:1

Am I currently someone that a child can look up to?

(Describe why or why not)

"Discipline your son, And he brings you
rest and delight to your life."

— Mashaly (Proverbs) 29:17

Do I have what it takes to raise a boy into a man?

(Describe why or why not)

"Do not profane your daughter by making her a whore, so that the land does not whore, and the land becomes filled with wickedness."

— Uyaqara (Leviticus) 19:29

Do I have what it takes to help raise a girl into a woman?

(Describe why or why not)

_____

_____

_____

_____

_____

_____

_____

_____

_____

_____

_____

_____

_____

_____

_____

_____

_____

"Rejoice, O young man, in your youth, and let your heart gladden you in the days of your youth. And walk in the ways of your heart, and in the sight of your eyes, but know that for all these Elohim brings you into right-ruling."

— Qahalath (Ecclesiastes) 11:9

What do I miss the most about my childhood?

(Describe your favorite memories)

"Folly is bound up in the heart of a child;
The rod of discipline drives it far from
him."

— Tahalym (Proverbs) 22:15

What do I hate the most about my childhood?

(Describe your worst memories)

"Fathers, do not provoke your children,
lest they become discouraged."

— Qolasym (Colossians) 3:21

What can I do to be a better father than my father was to me?

(Describe some different actions you can take)

_____

_____

_____

_____

_____

_____

_____

_____

_____

_____

_____

_____

_____

_____

_____

_____

_____

_____

_____

_____

_____

_____

"The wise one hears and increases learning, And the understanding one gets wise counsel."

— Tahalym (Proverbs) 5:1

Do I like learning new things?
(Describe why or why not)

_____

_____

_____

_____

_____

_____

_____

_____

_____

_____

_____

_____

_____

_____

_____

_____

_____

_____

_____

_____

"For whatever was written before was written for our instruction, that through endurance and encouragement of the Scriptures we might have the expectation."

— Romiyim (Romans) 15:4

What is my favorite method of learning?
(Describe why you like it)

"Learn to do good! Seek right-ruling, reprove the oppressor, defend the fatherless, plead for the widow."

— Yashayahu (Isaiah) 1:17

Did I learn anything about life or how to be a man in school?

(Describe your school experience)

"Ask and it shall be given to you, seek and you shall find, knock and it shall be opened to you."

— Mathathyahu (Matthew) 7:7

Am I willing to research and educate myself to learn how to be successful in life?

(Describe why or why not; if so, how)

"And to make it your ambition to live peaceably, and to attend to your own, and to work with your own hands, as we commanded you."

— 1 Tas'Loniqyim (Thessalonians) 4:11

Do I want to work for someone for a living or be self-employed?

(Describe why or why not)

_____

_____

_____

_____

_____

_____

_____

_____

_____

_____

_____

_____

_____

_____

_____

_____

_____

"The desire of the lazy man slays him, For his hands refused to work."

— Tahalym (Proverbs) 21:25

What could I do to earn a living for myself if I can't find a job?

(Describe what skills or talents you have)

"And יהוה Elohim took the man and put him in the garden of Eden to work it and to guard it."

— Barashyth (Genesis) 2:15

Am I prepared to grow my own food in the event I can no longer afford groceries?

(Describe your experience or lack thereof)

"And the food shall be for a store for the land for the seven years of scarcity of food which shall be in the land of Mitsrayim, and do not let the land be cut off by the scarcity of food."

— Barashyth (Genesis) 41:36

Do I have food stored up for myself and my family in case of a famine?

(Describe why you do or don't)

"My brothers, count it all joy when you fall into various trials, knowing that the proving of your belief works endurance."

— Yahqub (James) 1:2-3

Am I mentally tough enough to endure hard times?

(Describe your mental maturity level)

"I sought הוהי, and He answered me, And delivered me from all my fears."

— Mashaly (Psalms) 34:4

What is my biggest fear?
(Describe your fears)

"In Elohim I have trusted; I do not fear;
What could man do to me?"

— Mashaly (Psalms) 56:11

What would I do with my life if I wasn't so afraid?

(Express yourself)

_____

_____

_____

_____

_____

_____

_____

_____

_____

_____

_____

_____

_____

_____

_____

_____

_____

_____

_____

"For do I now persuade men, or Elohim?
Or do I seek to please men? For if I still
pleased men, I should not be a servant of
Messiah?"

— Galatiyim (Galatians) 1:10

Does it matter to me what people think about me?

(Describe why or why not)

_____

_____

_____

_____

_____

_____

_____

_____

_____

_____

_____

_____

_____

_____

_____

"Walk after הוהי your Elohim and fear Him, and guard His commands and obey His voice, and serve Him and cling to Him."

— Dabarym (Deuteronomy) 13:4

Am I living life to please myself, people, or The Most High?

(Describe who you live to please)

_____

_____

_____

_____

_____

_____

_____

_____

_____

_____

_____

_____

_____

_____

_____

_____

_____

_____

_____

_____

_____

"There was a man in the land of Uts, whose name was Iyob̲. And that man was perfect and straight, and one who feared Elohim and turned aside from evil."

— Ayub (Job) 1:1

What do I want people to remember or say about me when I die?

(Describe who you want your legacy to be)

"And do not fear those who kill the body but are unable to kill the being. But rather fear Him who is able to destroy both being and body in (Hell) Gehenna."

— Mathathyahu (Matthew) 10:28

If I died today, what do I think would happen to my soul?

(Describe the state of your soul)

"The voice of יהוה is with power, The voice of יהוה is with greatness."

— Mashaly (Psalms) 10:28

Am I connected to the Creator?

(Describe your relationship with The Most High)

_____

_____

_____

_____

_____

_____

_____

_____

_____

_____

_____

_____

_____

_____

_____

_____

_____

_____

_____

_____

_____

"Sing to Elohim, sing praises to His Name.
Raise up a highway for Him Who rides
through the deserts, By His Name Yah,
And exult before Him."

— Mashaly (Psalms) 68:4

What is the Creator's name?
(If you don't know, research it and write it down later)

"I, הוהי, search the heart, I try the kidneys, and give every man according to his ways, according to the fruit of his deeds."

— Yaramyahu (Jerimiah) 17:10

Do I think that YAH is pleased with the life that I have lived?

(Describe why or why not)

"If I have seen wickedness in my heart,
הוהי would not hear."

— Mashaly (Psalms) 66:18

What are the biggest obstacles holding me back from building a relationship with YAH?

(Describe what's in the way)

"And Kepha said to them, "Repent, and let each one of you be immersed in the Name of עשוהי Messiah for the forgiveness of sins. And you shall receive the gift of the Set-apart Spirit."

— Ma'asei (Acts) 2:38

How do I get my life right with YAH?
(Describe what you need to turn away from)

"Seek יהוה and His strength, Seek His face
continually!"

— 1 Yamym (Chronicles) 16:11

If I could write a letter to YAH, what would I tell him?

(Tell Him how you feel)

DIARY SECTION

(Express Yourself)

Share This Journal

If this journal has done its job and empowered you to become the man that YAH created you to be, then please *share this journal* with other young black men amongst your friends and family so it can do the same for them.

Also, please feel free to give this journal a review on **Amazon.com**. Your feedback is greatly appreciated and helps to inform our people of what this book is about.

We sincerely thank you for your support of this journal and pray that *The Most High* blesses you for blessing us. Shalom!

BLESSEDPRESS

Visit BlessedPress.com for more books.

About The Author

Maurice Lindsay, also known as Ma'orYahu, is a historian, writer, publisher and designer. As a writer and designer, Maurice loves creating literature and arts that inspire the African-American culture to grow. He is best known for his widespread blog, **TruthOverTradition.com**, where he shares untaught historical and biblical truths about the African Diaspora. He is also a youth mentor to at-risk teens in the urban communities. Maurice currently resides in South Carolina with his wife, Ashley, and their five children. For more information, visit *MauriceLindsay.com*.

- Maurice Lindsay

CPSIA information can be obtained
at www.ICGtesting.com
Printed in the USA
BVHW041050280519
549442BV00011B/194/P